table of contents

7 bewitching

14 easter sunday

22 wedding day

superheroes

28

34 nurse

2 head chef

10 cowgirl

19 luau

38 mermaid

head chef doll

Easy

MATERIALS

Yarn
RED HEART® Super Saver®, 7oz/198g skeins, each approx 364yd/333m (acrylic)
- 1 skein each in 316 Soft White (A), 520 Minty (B), 324 Bright Yellow (C), 334 Buff (D), 726 Coral (E), 400 Grey Heather (F), and 722 Pretty 'n Pink (G)

Hook
- Size I-9 (5.5mm) crochet hook, *or size to obtain gauge*

Notions
- Yarn needle
- Stitch marker
- 4 cardboard disks, one each 2"/5cm and 3"/7.5cm in diameter, two 4"/10cm in diameter
- Polyester fiberfill

FINISHED MEASUREMENTS
Dress fits 18"/45.5cm doll

GAUGE
12 sc = 4"/10cm; 15 rows = 4"/10cm using size I-9 (5.5mm) crochet hook.
CHECK YOUR GAUGE. Use any size hook to obtain the gauge.

SPECIAL STITCHES

Cl (double crochet cluster) Yarn over, insert hook in indicated stitch, yarn over and pull up loop, yarn over, draw through 2 loops on hook (2 loops remain on hook); [yarn over, insert hook in same stitch, yarn over and pull up loop, yarn over, draw through 2 loops] 3 times, yarn over, draw through all 5 loops on hook.

sc2tog [Insert hook in next stitch, yarn over and pull up a loop] twice, yarn over and draw through all 3 loops on hook.

sc3tog [Insert hook in next stitch, yarn over and pull up a loop] 3 times, yarn over and draw through all 4 loops on hook.

SPECIAL TECHNIQUE

Join with sc Place a slipknot on hook, insert hook in indicated stitch, yarn over and pull up a loop, yarn over and draw through both loops on hook.

NOTES

1) To change color, work last stitch of old color to last yarn over. Yarn over with new color and draw through all loops on hook to complete stitch. Proceed with new color. Cut old color.

2) Refer to photograph as a guide for placement of heart and pocket on apron.

OUTFIT

Hat
With A, ch 2.
Round 1 Work 6 sc in 2nd ch from hook; join with slip st in first sc—6 sc.
Round 2 Ch 1, 2 sc in each st around; join with slip st in first sc—12 sc.
Round 3 Ch 1, sc in first st, 2 sc in next st, *sc in next st, 2 sc in next st; repeat from * around; join with slip st in first sc—18 sc.
Round 4 Ch 1, sc in first 2 sts, 2 sc in next st, *sc in next 2 sts, 2 sc in next st; repeat from * around; join with slip st in first sc—24 sc.
Round 5 Ch 1, sc in first 3 sts, 2 sc in next st, *sc in next 3 sts, 2 sc in next st; repeat from * around; join with slip st in first sc—30 sc.
Round 6 Ch 1, sc in first 4 sts, 2 sc in next st, *sc in next 4 sts, 2 sc in next st; repeat from * around; join with slip st in first sc—36 sc.
Round 7 Ch 1, sc in first 5 sts, 2 sc in next st, *sc in next 5 sts, 2 sc in next st; repeat from * around; join with slip st in first sc—42 sc.
Round 8 Ch 1, sc in first 6 sts, 2 sc in next st, *sc in next 6 sts, 2 sc in next st; repeat from * around; join with slip st in first sc—48 sc.
Round 9 Ch 1, sc in first 7 sts, 2 sc in next st, *sc in next 7 sts, 2 sc in next st; repeat from * around; join with slip st in first sc—54 sc.
Round 10 Ch 1, sc in first 8 sts, 2 sc in next st, *sc in next 8 sts, 2 sc in next st; repeat from * around; join with slip st in first sc—60 sc.
Round 11 Ch 1, sc in first 9 sts, 2 sc in next st, *sc in next 9 sts, 2 sc in next st; repeat from * around; join with slip st in first sc—66 sc.
Round 12 Ch 1, sc in first 10 sts, 2 sc in next st, *sc in next 10 sts, 2 sc in next st; repeat from * around; join with slip st in first sc—72 sc.
Round 13 Ch 1, sc in first 11 sts, 2 sc in next st, *sc in next 11 sts, 2 sc in next st; repeat from * around; join with slip st in first sc—78 sc.

head chef doll

Round 14 Ch 1, sc in first 12 sts, 2 sc in next st, *sc in next 12 sts, 2 sc in next st; repeat from * around; join with slip st in first sc—84 sc.
Round 15 Ch 1, sc in first 13 sts, 2 sc in next st, *sc in next 13 sts, 2 sc in next st; repeat from * around; join with slip st in first sc—90 sc.
Round 16 Ch 1, sc in first 14 sts, 2 sc in next st, *sc in next 14 sts, 2 sc in next st; repeat from * around; join with slip st in first sc—96 sc.
Round 17 Ch 1, sc in first 15 sts, 2 sc in next st, *sc in next 15 sts, 2 sc in next st; repeat from * around; join with slip st in first sc—102 sc.
Round 18 Ch 1, sc in first 16 sts, 2 sc in next st, *sc in next 16 sts, 2 sc in next st; repeat from * around; join with slip st in first sc—108 sc.
Round 19 Ch 1, [sc3tog] around; join with slip st in first sc—36 sc.
Rounds 20–26 Ch 1, sc in each st around; join with slip st in first sc.
Fasten off.

Apron
With A, ch 19.
Row 1 Sc in 2nd ch from hook and in each remaining ch, turn—18 sc.
Rows 2–4 Ch 1, 2 sc in first sc, sc in each st across to last sc, 2 sc in last sc, turn—24 sc.
Rows 5–15 Ch 1, sc in each st across, turn.
Row 16 Ch 1, [sc2tog] twice, sc in each st across to last 4 sts, [sc2tog] twice, turn—20 sc.
Row 17 Ch 1, sc in each st across, turn.
Rows 18–21 Repeat Rows 16 and 17 twice—12 sc.
Row 22 Ch 1, sc2tog, sc in each st across to last 2 sts, sc2tog, turn—10 sc.
Rows 23–27 Ch 1, sc in each st across, turn. Do not turn at end of last row.
Row 28 **Ch 35, slip st in 2nd ch from hook and in each ch across (neck strap made)**; working in ends of rows of first side, sc evenly spaced across Rows 27–16, *ch 45, slip st in 2nd ch from hook and in each ch across (waist strap made)*, sc evenly spaced across Rows 15–2, 3 sc in Row 1; working in opposite side of foundation ch, sc in each ch across; working in ends of rows of other side, 3 sc in Row 1, sc evenly spaced across Rows 2–15; repeat from * to *, sc evenly spaced across Rows 16–27; repeat from ** to **, slip st in first sc of Row 27. Fasten off.

Heart
With B, ch 2.
Round 1 Work 6 sc in 2nd ch from hook; join with slip st in first sc—6 sc.
Round 2 Ch 3, 3 dc in first sc, 2 hdc in next sc, (2 sc, dc) in next sc, (dc, 2 sc) in next sc, 2 hdc in next sc, (3 dc, ch 3, slip st) in last sc. Fasten off, leaving a long tail for sewing. Sew heart to apron.

Pocket
With B, ch 7.
Row 1 Ch 1, sc in 2nd ch from hook and in ch across, turn—6 sc.
Row 2–5 Ch 1, 2 sc in first sc, sc in each st across to last sc, 2 sc in last sc, turn—14 sc.
Rows 6–11 Ch 1, sc in each st across, turn.
Fasten off, leaving a long tail for sewing.
Whipstitch pocket to apron.

BOWL

First Bottom Half
With C, work same as Rounds 1–4 of hat—24 sc. Fasten off.

Second Bottom Half
Rounds 1–4 Work same as first bottom half. At end of Round 4, do not fasten off. Holding first half on top of 2nd bottom half, place 2"/5cm disk between halves.
Round 5 Working through both thicknesses, repeat Round 5 of hat—30 sc.
Rounds 6 and 7 Ch 1, sc in each st around; join with slip st in first sc.
Round 8 Repeat Round 6 of hat—36 sc.

Rounds 9 and 10 Ch 1, sc in each st around; join with slip st in first sc.
Round 11 Repeat Round 7 of hat—42 sc.
Rounds 12–14 Ch 1, sc in each st around; join with slip st in first sc. Fasten off.

CHERRY PIE
Crust
With D, ch 12.
Row 1 (Wrong Side) Dc in 6th ch from hook (beginning skipped ch count as first dc, ch 1, skipped ch), *ch 1, skip next ch, dc in next ch; repeat from * across, turn—5 dc and 4 ch-1 spaces.
Row 2 Ch 4 (counts as dc, ch 1 here and throughout), dc in first dc, (ch 1, dc) in each dc across to beginning ch, [ch 1, dc] twice in 4th ch of beginning ch, turn—7 dc.
Row 3 Ch 4, dc in first dc, (ch 1, dc) in each dc across to beginning ch, [ch 1, dc] twice in 3rd ch of beginning ch, turn—9 dc.
Row 4 Ch 4, dc in next dc, (ch 1, dc) in each ch across to beginning ch, ch 1, dc in 3rd ch of beginning ch, turn.
Row 5 Ch 4, skip next dc, dc in next dc, (ch 1, dc) in next 4 dc, ch 1, skip last dc, dc in 3rd ch of beginning ch, turn—7 dc.
Row 6 Ch 4, skip next dc, dc in next dc, (ch 1, dc) in next 2 dc, ch 1, skip last dc, dc in 3rd ch of beginning ch—5 dc and 4 ch-1 spaces. Do not turn.
Border round Ch 1, working in ends of rows of first side, 3 sc in each row; working across opposite side of foundation ch, skip first ch-1 space, 3 sc in next 2 ch-1 spaces, skip last ch-1 space; working in ends of rows of other side, 3 sc in each row; working across top row, skip first ch-1 space, 3 sc in next 2 ch-1 spaces, skip last ch-1 space; join with slip st in first sc—48 sc. Fasten off.

Pie Filling
With E, work same as Rounds 1–8 of hat. Fasten off.

Pie Tin
First Bottom Half
With F, work same as Rounds 1–5 of hat—30 sc. Fasten off.

Second Bottom Half
Rounds 1–5 Work same as first bottom half. At end of Round 5, do not fasten off.
Hold first bottom half on top of 2nd bottom half, place 3"/7.5cm disk between halves.
Round 6 Working through both thicknesses, repeat Round 6 of hat—36 sc.
Rounds 7 and 8 Repeat Rounds 7 and 8 of hat—48 sc.
Round 9 Ch 1, sc in each st around; join with slip st in first sc. Fasten off.

Crust Edge
Place pie filling between pie tin and crust. Stuff with fiberfill between filling and tin as work progresses.
Round 1 Working through all 3 thicknesses, join D with sc in any st, (ch 5, sc) in each st around, ch 5; join with slip st in first st. Fasten off.

CAKE
Disk Covers (make 4)
With B, ch 2.
Rounds 1–6 Work same as Rounds 1–6 of hat—36 sc.
Round 7 Ch 1, sc in first 5 sts, 2 sc in next st, *sc in next 5 sts,

head chef doll

2 sc in next st; repeat from * around; change to G; join with slip st in first sc—42 sc.
Round 8 Ch 1, sc in each st around; join with slip st in first sc. Fasten off.

Sides
Place 4"/10cm disk between 2 disk covers.
Round 1 Working through both thicknesses, join G with sc in any st, Cl in same st, (sc, cl) in each st around; change to C; join with slip st in first sc, turn—42 sc and 42 Cls.
Round 2 Ch 1, sc in each sc around; change to B; join with slip st in first sc—42 sc.
Round 3 Ch 1, sc in each st around; join with slip st in first sc.
Round 4 Ch 1, sc in each st around; change to C; join with slip st in first sc.
Rounds 5–7 Repeats Rounds 2–4.
Round 8 Ch 1, sc in each st around; change to G; join with slip st in first sc.
Round 9 Ch 1, (sc, cl) in each st around; join with slip st in first sc. Fasten off.

Bottom of Cake
Stuff cake with fiberfill, then place last disk between remaining disk covers. Position covers on lower edge of sides. With G and working through all 3 thicknesses, whipstitch in each st around. Fasten off.

Candle
With G, ch 2.
Round 1 Work 5 sc in 2nd ch from hook—5 sc. Do not join until instructed. Place marker for beginning of round and move marker up as each round is completed.
Rounds 2–5 Sc in each sc around.
Rounds 6 Sc in each sc around; join with slip st in next st. Fasten off, leaving a long tail.

Flame
With C, ch 2.
Row 1 (Sc, ch 1, dc, ch 2, slip st in 2nd ch from hook, ch 1, sc) in 2nd ch from hook. Fasten off, leaving a long tail.
Sew flame to Round 1 of candle.
Sew candle to center of cake.

POT HOLDERS (make 2)
With G, ch 15.
Row 1 Sc in 2nd ch from hook and in each ch across, turn—14 sc.
Rows 2–4 Ch 1, sc in each st across, turn.
Row 5 Ch 1, sc in first 7 sts, Cl in next st, sc in last 6 sts, turn—13 sc and 1 Cl.
Row 6 Ch 1, sc in first 7 sts, skip next st, sc in last 6 sts, turn—13 sc.
Rows 7 and 8 Ch 1, sc in each st across, turn.
Row 9 Ch 1, sc in first st, [sc2tog] 6 times—7 sc. Fasten off, leaving a long tail.
Fold pot holder lengthwise and working through ends of rows and in sts last row, whipstitch edges together.

FINISHING
Weave in ends.•

bewitching doll

Easy

MATERIALS

Yarn
RED HEART® Super Saver®, 7oz/198g skeins, each approx 364yd/333m (acrylic)
• 1 skein each in 356 Amethyst (A), 722 Pretty 'n Pink (B), 254 Pumpkin (C), and 312 Black (D)

Hook
• Size G-6 (4.25mm) crochet hook, *or size to obtain gauge*

Notions
• Yarn needle
• Three ½"/12.7mm white buttons
• Stitch markers
• Sewing needle and white sewing thread

FINISHED MEASUREMENTS

Dress fits 18"/45.5cm doll

GAUGE

12 sts dc = 4"/10cm; 5 rows dc = 3"/7.5cm using size G-6 (4.25mm) crochet hook. *CHECK YOUR GAUGE. Use any size hook to obtain the gauge.*

SPECIAL ABBREVIATIONS

sc2tog (single crochet 2 together)
[Insert hook in next st, yarn over, draw up a loop] twice, yarn over, draw through 3 loops on hook.

DRESS

Bodice
Starting at neck edge with A, ch 25.
Row 1 (Right Side) Sc in 2nd ch from hook and each ch across; turn—24 sc.
Row 2 Ch 3 (counts as dc here and throughout), dc in first sc, 2 dc in each sc across; turn—48 dc.
Row 3 Ch 3, 2 dc in next dc, *dc in next st, 2 dc next st; repeat from * across; turn—72 dc.
Rows 4–6 Ch 3, dc in each dc across; turn.
Row 7 Ch 1, sc in first 9 dc, skip next 18 dc, sc in next 18 dc, skip next 18 dc, sc in last 9 dc; turn—36 sc.
Rows 8–10 Ch 1, sc in each sc across; turn.

Peplum
Row 11 Ch 3, working in back loops of sts, dc in very first sc, 2 dc in each st across; turn—72 dc.
Row 12 Ch 1, starting in first st, *sc in next 2 dc, 2 sc in next dc; repeat from * across; turn—96 sc.
Row 13 Ch 3, dc in each sc across; turn.
Row 14 *Ch 4, slip st in 2nd ch from hook, sc in next ch, dc in next ch, skip next 2 dc in row 13, slip st in next dc; repeat from * across—32 points. Fasten off.

Skirt
Row 15 With right side facing, working in remaining loops of sts in Row 10, join A with a slip st in front loop of first st, ch 3, dc in same st as joining, 2 dc in each st across; turn—72 dc.
Rows 16–26 Ch 3, dc in each dc across; turn.
Row 27 Ch 1, sc in each dc across; turn.

bewitching doll

Points
Row 28 Ch 1, starting in first st, *sc in each of next 6 sc, ch 1, turn, sc2tog over first 2 sts, sc in each of next 2 sc, sc2tog over first 2 sts, ch 1, turn, sc in each of next 4 sc, ch 1, turn, [sc2tog over first 2 sts] twice, ch 1, turn, sc2tog over first 2 sts, working in row-end sts, work 3 sc evenly spaced across side edge of point; repeat from * across—9 points. Fasten off, leaving a long sewing length.

ASSEMBLY
Sew back seam to 1"/2.5cm below waist. Sew Peplum seam. Evenly space 3 buttons on top left side of Back and sew in place with sewing needle and thread. Use spaces between sts on right Back for button holes.

HAT
With B, ch 2.
Round 1 6 sc in 2nd ch from hook; do not join—6 sc.
Work in a spiral, marking beginning of each round and moving marker up as work progresses.
Round 2 *Sc in next sc, 2 sc in next sc; repeat from * around—9 sc.
Round 3 Sc in each sc around.
Round 4 *Sc in each of next 2 sc, 2 sc in next sc; repeat from * around—12 sc.
Round 5 Sc in each sc around.
Round 6 *Sc in next sc, 2 sc in next sc; repeat from * around—18 sc.
Rounds 7 and 8 Sc in each sc around.
Round 9 *Sc in each of next 2 sc, 2 sc in next sc; repeat from * around—24 sc.
Rounds 10 and 11 Sc in each sc around.
Round 12 *Sc in each of next 3 sc, 2 sc in next sc; repeat from * around—30 sc.
Rounds 13 and 14 Sc in each sc around.
Round 15 *Sc in each of next 4 sc, 2 sc in next sc; repeat from * around—36 sc.
Rounds 16–18 Sc in each sc around.
Round 19 *Sc in each of next 5 sc, 2 sc in next sc; repeat from * around—42 sc.
Rounds 20 and 21 Sc in each sc around.
Round 22 *Sc in each of next 6 sc, 2 sc in next sc; repeat from * around—48 sc.
Fasten off B, join A.
Rounds 23–25 With A, sc in each sc around. Fasten off A, join B with slip st in front loop of first sc.
Round 26 With B, ch 3, working in front loops of sts, dc in first st, 2 dc in each st around; join with a slip st in top of beginning ch-3—96 dc.
Round 27 Ch 1, sc in each dc around; join with a slip st in first sc. Fasten off.

CAPE
Starting at neck edge with C, ch 78.
Row 1 Dc in 6th ch from hook, (beginning ch-5 counts as ch 1, dc, ch 1), *skip next 2 ch, 5 dc in next ch, skip next 2 ch, dc in next ch, ch 1, skip next ch, dc in next ch, rep from * across; turn—9 shells.
Row 2 Ch 4 (counts as dc, ch 1), skip next ch-1 space, dc in next dc, *skip next 2 dc, 5 dc in next dc, skip next 2 dc, dc in next dc, ch 1, skip next ch-1 space, dc in next dc; repeat from * across, ending with last dc in top of turning ch; turn. Fasten off C, join B.
Rows 3–10 Repeat Row 2, working in the following color sequence: *2 rows B, 2 rows C; repeat from * once. Fasten off C, join A.
Row 11 With A, repeat Row 2, do not turn. Do not fasten off.

Edging
Round 1 Working in row-end sts on side edge of Cape, sc evenly across to next corner, working across opposite side of foundation ch of neck, sc in each ch across, ch 1, turn, *sc2tog over next 2 sc; repeat from * across neck edge to next corner, turn, ch 40 (for tie), slip st in 2nd ch from hook, slip st in each ch across, sc in each st across neck edge to next corner, ch 40 (for tie), slip st in 2nd ch from hook, slip st in each ch across, working in row-end sts on other side edge, sc evenly across to next corner; join with slip st in top of beginning ch-3 of last row of cape. Fasten off.

PUMPKIN BAG
Starting at bottom edge with C, ch 12.
Round 1 Sc in 2nd ch from hook, sc in each of next 9 ch, 3 sc in last ch, working across opposite side of foundation ch, sc in each of next 9 ch, 2 sc in last ch; do not join—24 sc.
Work in a spiral, marking beginning of each round, moving marker up as work progresses.
Round 2 2 sc in next sc, sc in each of next 9 sc, 2 sc in each of next 3 sc, sc in each of next 9 sc, 2 sc in each of last 2 sc—30 sc.
Rounds 3–12 Sc in each sc around.
Round 13 *Sc in each of next 3 sc, sc2tog over next 2 sts; repeat from * around—24 sts.
Round 14 Sc in each of next 6 sc, ch 24 (for strap), skip next 6 sts, sc in each of next 6 sc, ch 24 (for strap), skip next 6 sts; join with a slip st in first sc. Fasten off C.
With D and yarn needle, following photo, embroider 2 vertical satin st eyes, horizontal satin st nose and back st mouth.

FINISHING
Weave in ends.•

cowgirl doll

Easy

MATERIALS

Yarn
RED HEART® With Love®, 7oz/198g skeins, each approx 370yd/338m (acrylic)
- 1 skein each 1101 Eggshell (A), 1308 Tan (B), 1401 Pewter (C), 1704 Bubble Gum (D), and 1805 Bluebell (E)

Hook
- Size I-9 (5.5mm) crochet hook, *or size to obtain gauge*

Notions
- Three ½"/12mm brown buttons for Shirt
- One ⅞"/22mm silver button for Belt
- One ½"/12mm decorative button or bead for Hat
- 4 mini pony beads for Hat
- Sewing needle and brown sewing thread
- Yarn needle
- Stitch markers

FINISHED MEASUREMENTS

Clothes fit 18"/45.5cm tall doll
Shirt (neck to bottom edge) 6"/15cm
Skirt (waist to bottom edge, with ruffle) 5"/12.5cm
Boots (height) 4"/10cm

GAUGE

12 sc = 4"/10cm; 15 rows sc = 4"/10cm using size I-9 (5.5mm) crochet hook.
CHECK YOUR GAUGE. Use any size hook to obtain the gauge.

NOTES

1) Use a stitch marker to keep track of beginnings of rounds.
2) Beginning ch-3 counts as a dc unless otherwise noted.

SPECIAL STITCHES

sc2tog (single crochet 2 together) [Draw up a loop in next st] twice, yarn over and draw through all 3 loops on hook.
dc2tog (double crochet 2 together) [Yarn over, insert hook in next stitch, yarn over and pull up loop, yarn over, draw through 2 loops] twice, yarn over, draw through all loops on hook.
dtr (double treble crochet) Yarn over three times, insert hook in next stitch, yarn over and pull up loop, [yarn over, draw through 2 loops] 4 times.

SPECIAL TECHNIQUE

Change color Work last stitch before changing color until 2 loops are left on hook (3 loops if working a sc2tog), complete stitch with new color. Cut first color unless otherwise noted.

HAT

Note Do not join rounds.
With B, ch 2.
Round 1 (Right Side) 8 sc in 2nd ch from hook—8 sc.
Round 2 2 sc in each sc—16 sc.
Round 3 *Sc in next sc, 2 sc in next sc; repeat from * around—24 sc.
Round 4 *Sc in each of next 2 sc, 2 sc in next sc; repeat from * around—32 sc.
Round 5 *Sc in each of next 7 sc, 2 sc in next sc; repeat from * around—36 sc.
Rounds 6–17 Sc in each sc around.
Round 18 Change color to C, do not cut B; sc in each sc around.
Round 19 Change color to B; working in front loops only, *sc in next sc, 2 sc in next sc; repeat from * around—54 sc.
Round 20 Working in both loops now and throughout, sc in each sc around.
Round 21 *Sc in each of next 2 sc, 2 sc in next sc; repeat from * around—72 sc.
Round 22 Sc in each sc around.
Round 23 *Sc in each of next 3 sc, 2 sc in next sc; repeat from * around—90 sc.
Round 24 Sc in each sc around.
Round 25 Slip st in each sc around—90 slip sts. Fasten off and weave in ends.

BOOTS (make 2)

With C, ch 7.
Round 1 (Right Side) 3 sc in 2nd ch from hook, sc in each of next 4 ch, 3 sc in last ch; turn piece upside down, working into opposite side of foundation ch, sc in each of next 4 ch; join with slip st in top of first sc—14sc.
Note Do not turn rounds.
Round 2 Ch 1, 2 sc in each of first 3 sc, sc in each of next 4 sc, 2 sc in

cowgirl doll

each of next 3 sc, sc in each of last 4 sc; join—20 sc.
Round 3 Ch 1; working in back loops only, sc in each sc around; join.
Round 4 Ch 1; working in both loops now and throughout, sc in each of first 10 sc, [sc2tog] 3 times, sc in each of last 4 sc; join—17 sts.
Round 5 Ch 1, sc in each of first 9 sts, [sc2tog], 3 times, sc in each of last 2 sc; join—14 sts.
Round 6 Ch 1, sc in each of first 10 sts, sc2tog, sc in each of last 2 sc; join—13 sts.
Rounds 7–11 Ch 1, sc in each st around; join—13 sc.
Round 12 Change color to A; ch 1, sc in each sc around; join—13 sc.
Round 13 Ch 1, sc in each sc around; join. Fasten off and weave in ends.

SHIRT
With B, ch 35.
Row 1 (Right Side) Dc in 4th ch from hook and in each ch across; turn—33 dc.
Rows 2–4 Ch 3, dc in each dc across; turn—33 dc.

Right Front
Row 5 Ch 3, dc in next 5 sts; turn—6 dc.
Row 6 Ch 3, dc in next 4 sts; turn—5 dc.
Row 7 Ch 3, dc in next 4 sts; turn—5 dc.
Row 8 Ch 3, dc in next 3 sts; turQ dc.
Row 9 Ch 3, dc2tog, dc; turn—3 sts.
Row 10 Ch 3, dc—2 dc. Fasten off and weave in ends.

Middle of Back
Row 5 With Right Side facing, skip next 6 unworked dc of Row 4. Attach B to next dc; ch 3, dc in next 8 dc; turn—9 dc.
Rows 6–8 Ch 3, dc in next 8 dc; turn—9 dc. At end of Row 8, do not turn. Fasten off and weave in ends.

Left Front
Rows 5–10 Attach B to top of last ch-3 of Row 4; repeat Rows 5–10 of Right Front.

Shoulders
Sew top of Right Front to top of first 2 sts of Middle of Back; fasten off and weave in ends. Sew top of Left Front to top of last 2 sts of Middle of Back; fasten off and weave in ends.

Front Edging
With Right Side facing, attach B to side post of Row 1; ch 1, 2 sc in each side post of Rows 1–10 of Right Front; sc in each of next 5 dc of Back; continuing around, 2 sc in each side post of Rows 10–1 of Left Front—45 sc. Fasten off and weave in ends.

Left Sleeve
Round 1 With Right Side facing, attach B to side post of Row 5 of Front; ch 1, 2 sc in each side post of Rows 5–10 of Front and Rows 8-5 of Back; working over next 6 dc of Row 4, [sc2tog] 3 times; join in top of first sc—23 sts.
Note Do not turn rounds.
Round 2 Change color to A; ch 1, working in back loops only, sc in each st around; join—23 sc.
Rounds 3–4 Ch 3; working in both loops now and throughout, dc in each sc around; join in top of ch-3—23 dc.
Round 5 Ch 1, [sc2tog, sc] 7 times, sc2tog; join in top of first sc2tog—15 sts.
Round 6 Ch 1, sc in each st around; join in top of first sc—15 sc. Fasten off and weave in ends.

Right Sleeve
Round 1 With Right Side facing, attach B to side post of Row 5 of Back; ch 1, 2 sc in each side post of Rows 5–8 of Back and Rows 10–5 of Front; working over next 6 dc of Row 4, [sc2tog] 3 times; join in top of first sc—23 sts.
Rounds 2–6 Repeat Rounds 2–6 of Left Sleeve, working without turning rounds.

BELT
With C, ch 40; dc in 4th ch from hook and in remaining chs—38 dc. Fasten off and weave in ends.

SKIRT
Note Do not join rounds.
With D, ch 32; being careful not to twist, join with slip st in first ch to form ring.
Round 1 (Right Side) Ch 1, sc in each ch; join with slip st in top of first sc—32 sc.
Round 2 Ch 3, dc in each of next 3 sc, [dtr in next sc, dc in each of next 7 sc] 3 times, dtr in next sc, dc in each of last 3 sc; join—28 dc, 4 dtr Belt Loops.

Rounds 3–7 Ch 3, dc in each st around; join—32 dc.

Front Ruffle
Round 8 Working in front loops only, ch 3, 3 dc in each st around; join—94 dc. Fasten off and weave in ends.

Back Ruffle
Round 9 Join A; working in back loops only, ch 3, 3dc in each st around; join—94 dc. Fasten off and weave in ends.

KERCHIEF
With E, ch 2.
Row 1 Sc in 2nd ch from hook; turn—1 sc.
Row 2 Ch 1, 3 sc in sc; turn—3 sc.
Row 3 Ch 1, 2 sc in first sc, sc in next sc, 2 sc in last sc; turn—5 sc.
Row 4 Ch 1, 2 sc in first sc, sc in each of next 3 sc, 2 sc in last sc; turn—7 sc.
Row 5 Ch 1, 2 sc in first sc, sc in each of next 5 sc, 2 sc in last sc; turn—9 sc.
Row 6 Ch 1, 2 sc in first sc, sc in each of next 7 sc, 2 sc in last sc; turn—11 sc.
Row 7 Ch 1, 2 sc in first sc, sc in each of next 9 sc, 2 sc in last sc; turn—13 sc.
Row 8 Ch 21, turn; slip st in 2nd ch from hook and next 19 ch, [sc in next sc, sc2tog] 4 times, sc in last sc—29 sts.
Row 9 Ch 21, turn; slip st in 2nd ch from hook and next 19 ch—20 slip sts. Fasten off and weave in ends.

FINISHING
Note Refer to photo for placement of items.
Hat
Push top of Hat inward, then tack Round 3 together. Tack side edges of Brim to sides of Round 16. Sew mini pony beads and decorative button to front of Hat.
Shirt
Sew three ½"/12mm brown buttons to Right Front of Shirt.
Belt
Sew ⅞"/22mm silver button to end of Row 1 of Belt. Slide Belt through Belt Loops of Skirt.•

easter sunday doll

Easy

MATERIALS

Yarn
RED HEART® Soft Baby Steps®, 5oz/141g balls, each approx 256yd/234m (acrylic)
- 1 ball each in 9200 Baby Yellow (A), 9505 Aqua (B), 9590 Lavender (C), 9600 White (D), 9630 Lime (E), 9700 Baby Pink (F), and 9702 Strawberry (G)

Hook
- Size F-5 (3.75mm) crochet hook, *or size to obtain gauge*

Notions
- Yarn needle
- Three ½"/12mm yellow buttons
- One ¾"/19mm white button
- Sewing needle and matching thread for buttons
- 3½"/9cm diameter cardboard circle
- Small amount of polyester fiberfill

FINISHED MEASUREMENTS
Clothes fit 18"/45.5cm doll.
Bodice (circumference) 12"/30.5cm
Dress (length) 11"/28cm
Headband (circumference) 12"/30.5cm
Egg basket (diameter) 4"/10cm

GAUGE
16 sts = 4"/10cm; 20 rows = 4"/10cm in single crochet using size F-5 (3.75mm) crochet hook.
CHECK YOUR GAUGE. Use any size hook to obtain the gauge.

SPECIAL STITCHES
bpdc (back post double crochet) Yarn over, insert hook from back side of work to front and to back again around the post of indicated stitch; yarn over and pull up a loop (3 loops on hook), yarn over and draw through 2 loops (2 loops on hook), yarn over and draw through 2 loops (1 loop on hook). Skip the stitch "in front of" the Bpdc.
fpdc (front post double crochet) Yarn over, insert hook from front side of work to back and to front again around post of indicated stitch; yarn over and pull up a loop (3 loops on hook), yarn over and draw through 2 loops (2 loops on hook), yarn over and draw through 2 loops (1 loop on hook).

SPECIAL TECHNIQUE
Join with sc Place a slipknot on hook, insert hook in indicated stitch, yarn over and draw up a loop, yarn over and draw through both loops on hook.

NOTES
1) Doll set consists of dress, headband, and basket of eggs.
2) Skirt is made from 36 granny squares sewn together. Each granny square is made in two sections of contrasting colors. Bodice is worked from top of skirt.
3) To change color, work last stitch of old color to last yarn over. Yarn over with new color and draw through all loops on hook to complete stitch. Proceed with new color. Cut old color.

DRESS
Skirt
Granny Squares (make 6 each with A, B, C, E, F, and G)
With A, ch 2.
Round 1 (Right Side) Work 6 sc in 2nd ch from hook; join with slip st in first sc; change to next color (except A), turn—6 sc.
Round 2 Ch 1, working in back loops only, 2 sc in each sc around; join with slip st in first sc—12 sc.
Round 3 Ch 2 (counts as first hdc), hdc in same st as join, hdc in next st, 2 hdc in next st, *ch 2, 2 hdc in next st, hdc in next st, 2 hdc in next st; repeat from * twice, ch 2; join with slip st in first hdc—20 hdc and 4 ch-2 spaces. Fasten off leaving a long tail for sewing.

Flowers (make 6 with A, 5 each with B, C, D, E, F, and G)
Petal Round Working in front loops only of Round 2, join any contrasting color with slip st to any st, *ch 5, skip next st, slip st in next st (petal made); repeat from * around ending last repeat in first slip st—6 petals. Fasten off.

Assembly
Arrange granny squares in 3 rows of 12 squares each, taking care that squares of the same color are not touching. Whipstitch squares together.

Bodice
Row 1 (Right Side) With Right Side of long edge facing, join D with sc in

easter sunday doll

ch-2 space at outer corner, *[skip next hdc, sc in next hdc] twice, skip next hdc, sc in next 2 ch-2 spaces; repeat from * 10 times, [skip next hdc, sc in next hdc] twice, skip last hdc, sc in last ch-2 space, turn—48 sc.
Rows 2 and 3 Ch 1, sc in each sc across, turn.
Row 4 Ch 1, sc in each sc across; change to A, turn.
Row 5 Ch 3 (counts as first dc here and throughout), dc in each st across, turn—48 dc.
Row 6 Ch 6, slip st in first dc (button loop made), ch 3, dc in each dc across to beginning ch, dc in top of beginning ch, turn—48 dc and 1 button loop.
Rows 7–9 Ch 3, dc in each dc across to beginning ch, dc in top of beginning ch, turn.

Right Back
Row 10 (Wrong Side) Ch 6, slip st in first dc (button loop made), ch 3, dc in next 8 dc; leave remaining sts unworked, turn—9 dc and 1 button loop.
Rows 11–13 Repeat Rows 7–9.
Row 14 Ch 6, slip st in first dc (button loop made), ch 3, dc in next 8 dc. Fasten off, leaving a long tail for sewing.

Front
Row 10 (Wrong Side) With Wrong Side facing, skip next 6 unworked sts of Row 9, join A with slip st to next dc, ch 3, dc in next 4 dc, hdc in next 2 dc, sc in next 4 dc, hdc in next 2 dc, dc in last 5 dc, turn—18 sts.
Rows 11–14 Ch 3, dc in next 4 dc, hdc in next 2 dc, sc in next 4 dc, hdc in next 2 dc, dc in last 4 dc, dc in top of beginning ch, turn. Fasten off.

Left Back
Row 10 (Wrong Side) With Wrong Side facing, skip next 6 unworked sts of Row 9, join A with slip st to next dc, ch 3, dc in remaining 8 dc, turn—9 dc.
Rows 11–14 Repeat Row 5.
Fasten off, leaving a long tail for sewing.

Assembly
Left Shoulder
With Wrong Sides held together, whipstitch last 5 dc of left back to first 5 dc of front.

Right Shoulder
With Wrong Sides held together, whipstitch last 5 dc of front to first 5 dc of right back.

Left Shoulder Ruffle
Row 1 (Right Side) With Right Side of left front facing and working in ends of rows, join D with sc in Row 10, sc in same row, 2 sc in Rows 11–14 of left front and in Rows 14–10 of left back, turn—20 sc.
Row 2 Ch 1, 2 sc in first 2 sc, 2 hdc in next 2 sc, 2 dc in next 12 sc, 2 hdc in next 2 sc, 2 sc in last 2 sc, turn—40 sts.
Row 3 Ch 1, 2 sc in first 4 sc, 2 hdc in next 4 hdc, 2 dc in next 24 dc, 2 hdc in next 4 hdc, 2 sc in last 4 sc—80 sts. Fasten off.

Right Shoulder Ruffle
Row 1 (Right Side) With Right Side of right back facing and working in ends of rows, join D with sc in Row 10, sc in same row, 2 sc in Rows 11–14 of right back and in Rows 14–10 of right front, turn—20 sc.
Rows 2 and 3 Repeat Rows 2 and 3 of left shoulder ruffle.

Skirt Ruffle
Row 1 (Right Side) With Right Side of lower edge of skirt facing, join D with slip st in first ch-2 space at outer corner, ch 3, dc in same ch-2 space, 2 dc in each hdc and ch-2 space across, turn—168 dc.
Row 2 Ch 3, 2 dc in next dc, *dc in next dc, 2 dc in next dc; repeat from * across working last dc in top of beginning ch, turn—252 dc.
Row 3 Ch 3, dc in each dc across to beginning ch, dc in top of beginning ch. Fasten off, leaving long tail for sewing. Whipstitch back of skirt together.

Bow Straps (make 2)
With D, ch 60, dc in 4th ch from hook (beginning ch count as first dc here and throughout) and in each ch across—58 dc. Fasten off, leaving long tail for sewing.

FINISHING DRESS
With Right Side of bodice facing, sew first st of each bow strap to ends of Rows 1–4 at each edge.
With Right Side facing, sew ½"/12mm buttons to left edge

opposite button loops.
Weave in ends.

HEADBAND
With D, ch 51.
Row 1 (Right Side) Sc in 2nd ch from hook and in each ch across, turn—50 sc.
Rows 2–4 Ch 1, sc in each sc across, turn.
Row 5 Ch 1, sc in each sc across, ch 5; join with slip st in first sc of Row 1 (button loop made). Fasten off.

Bunny Ears (make 2)
Front
With F, ch 13.
Row 1 (Right Side) Dc in 4th ch from hook, dc in next 9 ch, 5 dc in last ch; working in opposite side of foundation ch, skip first ch, dc in next 10 ch—25 dc. Fasten off.

Back
Row 1 With D, repeat Row 1 of front. Do not fasten off.
Row 2 With Wrong Sides of front and back held together and working through both thicknesses, ch 1, sc in first 4 dc, hdc in next 4 dc, dc in next 4 dc, (2 dc, ch 3, slip st in 2nd ch from hook) in next st, dc in next 4 dc, hdc in next 4 dc, sc in last 4 dc. Fasten off, leaving long tail for sewing.

FINISHING HEADBAND
Place headband on doll for button placement. Sew ¾"/19mm button in place.
Referring to photo for placement, sew ears to headband.
Weave in all ends.

BASKET
Cover (make 1 each with E and G)
Ch 2.
Round 1 Work 6 sc in 2nd ch from hook; join with slip st in first sc—6 sc.
Round 2 Ch 1, 2 sc in each sc around; join with slip st in first sc—12 sc.
Round 3 Ch 1, sc in first sc, 2 sc in next sc, *sc in next sc, 2 sc in next sc; repeat from * around; join with slip st in first sc—18 sc.
Round 4 Ch 1, sc in first 2 sc, 2 sc in next sc, *sc in next 2 sc,

2 sc in next sc; repeat from * around; join with slip st in first sc—24 sc.
Round 5 Ch 1, sc in first 3 sc, 2 sc in next sc, *sc in next 3 sc, 2 sc in next sc; repeat from * around; join with slip st in first sc—30 sc.
Round 6 Ch 1, sc in first 4 sc, 2 sc in next sc, *sc in next 4 sc, 2 sc in next sc; repeat from * around; join with slip st in first sc—36 sc.
Round 7 Ch 1, sc in first 5 sc, 2 sc in next sc, *sc in next 5 sc, 2 sc in next sc; repeat from * around; join with slip st in first sc—42 sc.
Round 8 Ch 1, sc in first 6 sc, 2 sc in next sc, *sc in next 6 sc, 2 sc in next sc; repeat from * around; join with slip st in first sc—48 sc. Fasten off.

Body

Rounds 1–8 With G, work same as Rounds 1–8 of top base. Place cardboard circle on top of Rounds 1–8, place G-colored cover on top of cardboard circle.
Round 9 Ch 3, working through both thicknesses, dc in each st around; join with slip st in top of beginning ch—48 dc.
Round 10 Ch 3, fpdc around next 3 sts, bpdc around next 4 sts, *fpdc around next 4 sts, bpdc around next 4 sts; repeat from * around; join with slip st in top of beginning ch.
Rounds 11 and 12 Ch 3, bpdc around next 3 sts, fpdc around next 4 sts, *bpdc around next 4 sts, fpdc around next 4 sts; repeat from * around; join with slip st in top of beginning ch.
Rounds 13 and 14 Repeat Round 10.

Stuff lightly with fiberfill.
Round 15 Place E-colored cover (grass) in basket, ch 1, working through both thicknesses, sc in each st around; join with slip st in first sc. Fasten off.

Easter Eggs (make 1 each with A, C, and F, 2 with B)
Ch 2.
Round 1 Work 6 sc in 2nd ch from hook; join with slip st in first sc—6 sc.
Round 2 Ch 1, sc in first 2 sc, 2 sc in next sc, sc in next 2 sc, 2 sc in last sc; join with slip st in first sc—8 sc.
Round 3 Ch 1, sc in first 3 sc, 2 sc in next sc, sc in next 3 sc, 2 sc in last sc; join with slip st in first sc—10 sc.
Round 4 Ch 1, sc in first 4 sc, 2 sc in next sc, sc in next 4 sc, 2 sc in last sc; join with slip st in first sc—12 sc.
Round 5 Ch 1, sc in first 5 sc, 2 sc in next sc, sc in next 5 sc, 2 sc in last sc; join with slip st in first sc—14 sc. Fasten off, leaving a long tail for sewing.

FINISHING BASKET
Stuff each egg lightly with fiberfill. Weave tail through last round and pull gently to close slightly. Sew to grass.

Grass Strands

Cut 30 strands of E, each 3"/7.5cm long. Fold strand in half to form a loop. Insert crochet hook around any st of grass. Place fold on hook and draw fold through, forming a loop. Thread ends of strand through loop and pull to tighten. Repeat to attach grass strands last in spaces between Easter eggs. Trim ends to desired length.

Handle

With G, leaving a long tail for sewing, ch 6.
Row 1 Dc in 4th ch from hook and in each ch across, turn—4 dc.
Rows 2–21 Ch 3, dc in each dc across to beginning ch, dc in top of beginning ch, turn.
Fasten off, leaving a long tail for sewing.
Referring to photograph as a guide, sew handle to opposite sides of Round 15.
Weave in ends.•

luau doll

Easy

MATERIALS
Yarn
RED HEART® Super Saver®, 7oz/198g skeins, each approx 364yd/333m (acrylic)
- 1 skein each in 373 Petal Pink (A), 324 Bright Yellow (B), 254 Pumpkin (C), and 722 Pretty 'N Pink (D)

RED HEART® Scrubby™, 3½oz/100g balls, each approx 92yd/85m (polyester)
- 1 ball in 620 Lime (E)

Hook
- Size I-9 (5.5mm) crochet hook, *or size to obtain gauge*

Notions
- 21 mini white pony beads
- 4 snaps
- Yarn needle
- Sewing needle and sewing thread

FINISHED MEASUREMENTS
Dress fits 18"/45.5cm doll

GAUGE
12 sc = 4"/10cm; 15 rows sc = 4"/10cm using size I-9 (5.5mm) crochet hook. *CHECK YOUR GAUGE. Use any size hook to obtain the gauge.*

NOTE
Ch-1 at beginning of row does not count as a separate stitch.

TOP
With A, ch 35.
Row 1 (Wrong Side) Sc in 2nd ch from hook and each remaining ch; turn—34 sc.
Row 2 Ch 1, sc in each sc; turn.
Rows 3–10 Repeat Row 2.

Left Back
Row 11 Ch 1, sc in first 6 sc; leave remaining sc unworked; turn—6 sc.
Rows 12–17 Repeat Row 11; fasten off.

Right Back
Referring to photo for placement, attach A to first sc of Row 11; repeat Rows 11–17 of Left Back.

Front
Row 11 Referring to photo for placement, attach A to 6th unworked st of Row 10; ch 1, sc in same attached st and next 11 sc; turn—12 sc.
Row 12 Ch 1, sc in first 12 sc; turn.

Left Front
Row 13 Ch 1, sc in first 6 sc; turn—6 sc.
Row 14 Ch 1, skip first sc; sc in remaining 5 sc; turn—5 sc.
Row 15 Ch 1, sc in first 5 sc; turn—5 sc.
Row 16 Ch 1, skip first sc, sc in remaining 4 sc; turn—4 sc.
Row 17 Ch 1, sc in first 4 sc; turn—4 sc.
Row 18 Ch 1, skip first sc, sc in remaining 3 sc; turn—3 sc.
Row 19 Ch 1, sc in first 3 sc; fasten off, leaving long tail for finishing—3 sc.

luau doll

Right Front
Row 13 Referring to photo for placement, attach A to first sc of Row 12 of Front; repeat Rows 13–19 of Left Front.

WRIST FLOWERS (make 2 each with B, C, and D)
Ch 4; join with slip st to form ring.
Row 1 *Ch 4, slip st in ring; repeat from * 4 more times; fasten off, leaving long tail for finishing—5 ch-4 loops.

HEADBAND FLOWERS (make 5 each with B, C, and D)
Ch 4; join with slip st to form ring.
Row 1 *Ch 2 (counts as first dc), dc in ring, ch 2, slip st in ring; repeat from * 4 more times; fasten off, leaving long tail for finishing—5 Petals.

LEI FLOWERS (make 17 each with B, C, and D)
Repeat Headband Flower. Instead of leaving long tail for finishing, weave in ends.

LEI LACE
With A, and leaving long tails at beginning and end of work, ch 50; fasten off.

WRISTBAND
With A, ch 12.
Row 1 Sc in 2nd ch from hook and remaining chs; fasten off, leaving long tail for finishing—11 sc.

HEADBAND
With A, ch 38.
Row 1 Dc in 4th ch from hook (counts as first 2 dc) and remaining chs; fasten off, leaving long tail for finishing—36 dc.

FINISHING
Outfit
Referring to photo for placement, use long tails of Front pieces to sew Left Front and Right Front pieces to the first 3 sts nearest to the armholes of both sides of the Back; weave in ends. Sew snaps to edges of Back.

Skirt Fringe
With E, cut 136 strands, each 14"/35.5cm long, for fringe. Holding 4 strands together, fold in half. Referring to photo for placement, attach each group to the back of each st of the foundation ch—thirty-four 7"/18cm fringes made.

Wrist Flowers
Using a long tail, sew one pony bead to middle of a Flower; using same long tail, sew Flower to Wristband. Repeat for each Flower; weave in all ends.

Headband
Using a long tail, sew one pony bead to middle of a Flower; using same long tail, sew Flower to Headband. Repeat for each Flower; weave in all ends.

Lei
String all Lei Flowers on Lei Lace; tie Lace ends together.•

wedding day doll

Experienced

MATERIALS

Yarn
AUNT LYDIA'S® Classic Crochet Thread, Size 10, each approx 400yd/366m (mercerized cotton)
- 2 balls in 001 White

Hook
Size 6 (1.6mm) steel crochet hook, *or size to obtain gauge*

Notions
- 1161 White 4mm pearl beads (741 for Dress, 270 for Flowers, 30 for Neck, 120 for Collar)
- 33yd/30m white tulle fabric, 6"/15cm wide
- Five ½"/12mm white buttons
- White sewing thread
- Beading needle
- Tapestry needle
- Stitch markers

FINISHED MEASUREMENTS

Dress fits 18"/45.5cm tall doll
Dress (neck to lower edge) 13"/33cm
Underskirt (length) 9½"/24cm

GAUGE

(Dc, ch 2) 14 times = 4"/10 cm; 16 rows dc = 4"/10cm using size 6 (1.6mm) steel crochet hook.
CHECK YOUR GAUGE. Use any size hook to obtain the gauge.

SPECIAL STITCHES

V-st (Dc, ch 2, dc) in indicated stitch or space.
Shell ([Dc, ch 2] 3 times, dc) in indicated stitch or space.
Shell in Shell Shell in center chain-2 space of indicated Shell; do not work into the other 2 chain-2 spaces of the Shell.
Shell in V-st Shell in chain-2 space of indicated V-st.
dc2tog (double crochet 2 together) [Yarn over, insert hook in indicated stitch or space and draw up a loop, yarn over and draw through 2 loops on hook] twice, yarn over and draw through all 3 loops on hook.
dc3tog (double crochet 3 together) [Yarn over, insert hook in indicated stitch or space and draw up a loop, yarn over and draw through 2 loops on hook] 3 times, yarn over and draw through all 4 loops on hook.

SPECIAL TECHNIQUES

Adjustable Ring Wrap thread into a ring, ensuring that the tail falls behind the working thread. Grip ring and tail firmly between middle finger and thumb. Insert hook through center of ring, yarn over (with working thread) and draw up a loop. Work stitches of first round in the ring. After the first round of stitches is worked, pull gently, but firmly, on tail to tighten ring.
Join with sc Place a slipknot on hook, insert hook in indicated stitch or space, yarn over and draw up a loop, yarn over and draw through both loops on hook.
Bring up bead(s) Slide the indicated number of beads up the thread next to the last stitch made. Beads are drawn up while working wrong side rows/rounds, but will show on the right side.
String beads Cut a length of sewing thread and fold it in half, bringing both ends together and forming a loop. Thread the two ends into eye of beading needle. Place end of crochet thread into loop. Pick up each bead with tip of beading needle, slide bead over sewing thread and onto crochet thread.

NOTES

1) Dress is worked in two sections: Skirt and Bodice. The skirt is worked from the waist down to the lower edge and the bodice is worked from the waist up to the neck edge.
2) An underskirt and veil are worked separately. Each consists of a crocheted band to which lengths of tulle are attached.
3) Beaded flowers are worked separately and sewn to the dress and veil.

DRESS

Skirt
Row 1 Ch 5, slip st in 5th ch from hook (first ch-loops made) *ch 5, slip st in 5th ch from hook; repeat from * until you have a total of 38 ch-loops. Hold strip of ch-spaces just made with the slip sts at the top.
Row 2 Ch 1, sc in last ch-space made, [ch 3, sc in next ch-space] 37 times, turn—38 sc and 37 ch-3 spaces.
Row 3 (waistband) Ch 6 (counts as first dc and ch-3 space), skip first ch-3 space, dc in next sc, [ch 3, skip next ch-3 space, dc in next sc] 36 times—38 dc, 37 ch-3 spaces.
Note The piece is now joined into a circle and work proceeds in rounds. Do not join at ends of rounds, work in continuous rounds (spiral), until instructed.

wedding day doll

Round 4 Taking care not to twist piece, dc in 3rd ch of Row 3 beginning ch-6 to begin working in rounds, place a marker in dc just made for beginning of round, move marker up as each round is started ch 2, skip next ch-3 space, V-st in next dc, [ch 2, skip next ch-3 space, dc in next dc, ch 2, skip next ch-3 space, V-st in next dc] 18 times, ch 2—19 dc and 19 V-sts.

Round 5 [Dc in next dc, ch 2, V-st in next V-st, ch 2] 19 times.

Round 6 [Dc in next dc, ch 3, V-st in next V-st, ch 3] 19 times.

Round 7 [Dc in next dc, Shell in next V-st] 19 times—19 dc and 19 Shells.

Round 8 [Dc in next dc, Shell in Shell] 19 times.

Rounds 9 and 10 [Dc in next dc, ch 1, Shell in Shell, ch 1] 19 times.

Rounds 11–13 [Dc in next dc, ch 2, Shell in Shell, ch 2] 19 times.

Round 14 [Dc in next dc, ch 1, dc in next ch-2 space, ch 2, Shell in Shell, ch 2, dc in next ch-2 space, ch 1] 19 times—57 dc and 19 Shells.

Round 15 [Dc in next dc, ch 2, skip next ch-1 space, dc in next ch-2 space, ch 2, Shell in Shell, ch 2, dc in next ch-2 space, ch 2, skip next ch-1 space] 19 times.

Round 16 *Dc in next dc, [dc in next ch-2 space, ch 2] twice, Shell in Shell, [ch 2, dc in next ch-2 space] twice; repeat from * 18 more times—95 dc and 19 Shells.

Round 17 *Dc in next dc, ch 1, [dc in next ch-2 space, ch 2] twice, Shell in Shell, [ch 2, dc in next ch-2 space] twice, ch 1, skip next dc; repeat from * 18 more times.

Round 18 *Dc in next dc, ch 2, skip next ch-1 space, [dc in next ch-2 space, ch 2] twice, Shell in Shell, [ch 2, dc in next ch-2 space] twice, ch 2; repeat from * 18 more times.

Round 19 *Dc in next dc, [dc in next ch-2 space, ch 2] 3 times, Shell in Shell, [ch 2, dc in next ch-2 space] 3 times; repeat from * 18 more times—133 dc and 19 Shells.

Round 20 *Dc in next dc, ch 1, [dc in next ch-2 space, ch 2] 3 times, Shell in Shell, [ch 2, dc in next ch-2 space] 3 times, ch 1, skip next dc; repeat from * 18 more times.

Round 21 *Dc in next dc, ch 2, skip next ch-1 space, [dc in next ch-2 space, ch 2, skip next dc] 3 times, Shell in Shell, [ch 2, dc in next ch-2 space] 3 times, ch 2, skip next ch-1 space; repeat from * 18 more times.

Round 22 *Dc in next dc, [dc in next ch-2 space, ch 2] 4 times, Shell in Shell, [ch 2, dc in next ch-2 space] 4 times; repeat from * 18 more times—171 dc and 19 Shells.

Round 23 *Dc in next dc, ch 1, [dc in next ch-2 space, ch 2] 4 times, Shell in Shell, [ch 2, dc in next ch-2 space] 4 times, ch 1, skip next dc; repeat from * 18 more times.

Round 24 *Dc in next dc, ch 2, skip next ch-1 space, [dc in next ch-2 space, ch 2] 4 times, Shell in Shell, [ch 2, dc in next ch-2 space] 4 times, ch 2; repeat from * 18 more times.

Round 25 *Dc in next dc, [dc in next ch-2 space, ch 2] 5 times, Shell in Shell, [ch 2, dc in next ch-2 space] 5 times; repeat from * 18 more times, join with slip st in first dc of this round—209 dc and 19 Shells.

Round 26 Ch 3, dc2tog over first 2 dc (beginning ch-3 and dc2tog count as first dc3tog here and at beginning of next round), *ch 2, skip next ch-2 space, [dc in next ch-2 space, ch 2] 4 times, Shell in Shell, [ch 2, dc in next ch-2 space] 4 times, ch 2, skip next ch-2 space**, dc3tog over next 3 dc; repeat from * around, ending last repeat at **; join with slip st in top of beginning ch-3—152 dc, 19 Shells and 19 dc3tog.

Round 27 Ch 3, dc2tog over first dc3tog and next ch-2 space, *ch 2, [dc in next ch-2 space, ch 2] 4 times, Shell in Shell, [ch 2, dc in next ch-2 space] 4 times, ch 2**, dc3tog over next ch-2 space, next dc3tog, and next ch-2 space; repeat from * around,

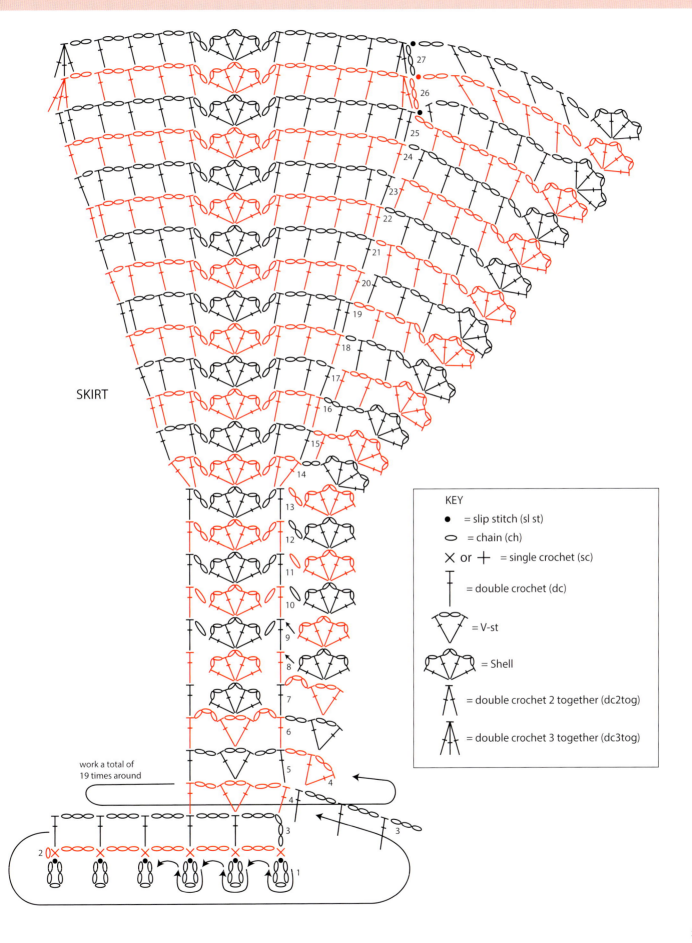

wedding day doll

ending last repeat at **; join with slip st in top of beginning ch-3—247 ch-2 spaces (including ch-2 spaces within the Shells). Fasten off.

Skirt Edging
String 741 beads.
With wrong side facing, join thread with sc in any ch-2 space, sc in same ch-2 space, bring up 3 beads, *ch 1, 2 sc in next ch-2 space, bring up 3 beads; repeat from * around, ch 1; join with slip st in first sc—494 sc and 247 groups of 3 beads. Fasten off.

BODICE
String 120 beads (for use when making the collar).
With Right Side of skirt facing and Row 1 at top, join thread with slip st in first ch-loop.
Row 1 (Right Side) Ch 3 (counts as first dc here and throughout), (dc, ch 1, dc) in same ch-loop as joining, *ch 1, dc in next ch-loop repeat from * to last ch-loop, ch 1, (dc, ch 1, 2 dc) in last ch-loop, turn—42 dc and 39 ch-1 spaces.
Row 2 Ch 3, V-st in first ch-1 space, *ch 1, skip next ch-1 space, V-st in next ch-1 space; repeat from * across; dc in top of beginning ch-3, turn—2 dc and 20 V-sts.
Rows 3–5 Ch 3, V-st in next V-st, *ch 1, V-st in next v-st; repeat from * across, dc in top of beginning ch-3, turn.
Row 6 (Shape Armholes) Ch 3, V-st in next V-st, [ch 1, V-st in next V-st] 3 times, ch 3, 2 sc in next V-st, 2 sc in next ch-1 space between V-sts, 2 sc in next V-st, ch 3, V-st in next V-st, [ch 1, V-st in next V-st] 7 times, ch 3, 2 sc in next V-st, 2 sc in next ch-1 space between V-sts, 2 sc in next V-st, ch 3, V-st in next V-st, [ch 1, V-st in next V-st] 3 times, dc in last dc, turn—2 dc, 16 V-sts, 12 sc, and 4 ch-3 spaces.
Row 7 Ch 3, V-st in next V-st, [ch 1, V-st in next V-st] 3 times, ch 15, skip next 2 ch-3 spaces, V-st in next V-st, [ch 1, V-st in next V-st] 7 times, ch 15, skip next 2 ch-3 spaces, V-st in next V-st, [ch 1, V-st in next V-st] 3 times, dc in last dc, turn—2 dc, 16 V-sts, and 2 ch-15 spaces. Do not fasten off.

Collar
Row 1 Ch 1, sc in first dc, [2 sc in next V-st, sc in next ch-1 space between V-sts] 3 times, 2 sc in next V-st, 17 sc in next ch-15 space, [2 sc in next V-st, sc in next ch-1 space between V-sts] 7 times, 2 sc in next V-st, 17 sc in next ch-15 space, [2 sc in next V-st, sc in next ch-1 space] 3 times, 2 sc in next V-st, sc in last dc, turn—81 sc.
Row 2 Ch 1, sc in first sc, *ch 5, skip next sc, sc in next sc; repeat from * across, turn—40 ch-5 spaces.
Row 3 Ch 7, sc in first ch-5 space, *ch 5, sc in next ch-5 space; repeat from * across, tur 0 ch-spaces (including the beginning ch-7 space).
Rows 4 and 5 Ch 8, sc in first ch-space, *ch 6, sc in next ch-space; repeat from * across, turn.
Row 5 Ch 8, sc in first ch-space, *ch 6, sc in next ch-space; repeat from * across, turn.
Rows 6 and 7 Ch 9, sc in first ch-space, *ch 7, sc in next ch-space; repeat from * across, turn.
Row 8 Ch 10, sc in first ch-space, *ch 8, sc in next ch-space; repeat from * across, turn.
Row 9 Ch 3, (3 dc, bring up 3 beads, ch 1, 3 dc) in each ch-space across—Forty 3-dc groups and 40 groups of 3 beads. Fasten off.

NECK EDGING AND BACK BANDS
Notes Neck edging and back bands are worked at the same time. Round 1 is worked in one continuous round across the neck, down the right back edge then up the left back edge. Row 2 is worked across the neck only. The piece is then turned and Round 3 is worked across the neck, down the left back edge, and up the right back edge.

String 30 beads.
Fold collar down over bodice so that right side of collar is facing out.
Round 1 (Right Side) Working in the unworked sc sts of Row 1 of collar (these are the sc sts that were skipped when Row 2 of collar was worked), join thread with sc in first unworked sc, sc in same sc,*sc in next unworked sc, 2 sc in next unworked sc; repeat from * across to last unworked sc, 2 sc in last unworked sc; work 20 dc evenly spaced down right side edge of back opening, then 20 dc evenly spaced up left side edge of back opening; join with slip st in first sc, do not turn—61 sc and 40 dc.
Row 2 Ch 1, sc in next 61 sc across neck only, turn, leaving remaining sts unworked—61 sc.
Round 3 (Wrong Side) Ch 1, sc in first sc, [bring up bead, ch 1, skip next sc, sc in next sc] 30 times; ch 1, working down left side edge of back opening, slip st in end of Row 2, [ch 3, skip next 2 dc, slip st in next 6 dc] twice, ch 3, skip next 2 dc, slip st in next 2 dc; working up right side edge of back opening, slip st in next 2 dc, [ch 3, skip next 2 dc, slip st in next 6 dc] twice, ch 3, skip next 2 dc, slip st in end of Row 2; join with slip st in first sc. Fasten off.

UNDERSKIRT
Band
Ch 8.

BODICE

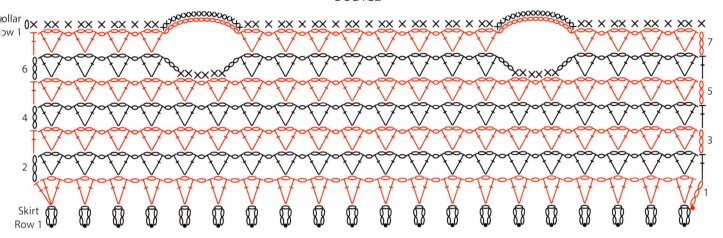

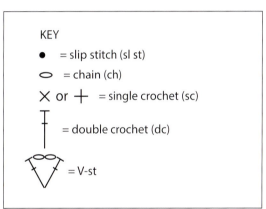

Row 1 (Right Side) Dc in 4th ch from hook (3 skipped ch count as first dc), [skip next ch, 2 dc in next ch] twice, turn—Three 2-dc groups.
Rows 2–40 Ch 3 (counts as dc here and throughout), dc in space between first 2 dc, skip next 2 dc, 2 dc in next space between sts, skip next 2 dc, 2 dc in space between last dc and beginning ch, turn. Band should measure about 10½"/26.5cm without stretching.
Buttonhole Row Ch 1, 2 sc in space between first 2 dc, ch 3, 2 sc in space between last dc and beginning ch. Fasten off.

Attach Tulle
Cut 40 lengths of tulle 22"/56cm long.
Fold one length in half, forming a loop at folded end. Draw loop through one end of Row 1 of band, thread ends of tulle through loop and pull to tighten and secure. Repeat to attach a length of tulle to the same end of each row of band. Lay underskirt on table and trim ends to about 9"/23cm.

VEIL
Band
Work veil band same as underskirt band.
Attach Tulle
Cut 10 lengths of tulle 24"/61cm long. Attach one length to center V-st of Rows 1, 3, 5, 7, 9, 32, 34, 36, 38, and 40.

BEADED FLOWERS (make 45—38 for dress, 7 for veil)
String 6 beads. Leaving a long tail to sew flower to dress, make an adjustable ring.
Round 1 (Wrong Side) Ch 1, [sc in ring, bring up bead, ch 1] 6 times; join with slip st in first sc, turn—6 sc and 6 beads.

Round 2 [Ch 5, slip st in next sc] 5 times, ch 5; join with slip st in beginning slip st—6 ch-5 loops. Fasten off.

FINISHING
Attach Flowers
Referring to photos for placement, sew one flower about 1"/2.5cm above each point at lower edge of skirt. Sew 19 flowers evenly spaced around skirt about 3"/7.5cm below Row 3 (waist). Sew 7 flowers evenly spaced across front of veil.
Attach Buttons
Sew buttons over the 3 ch-3 spaces on one side of back band, use the ch-3 spaces on the other side of back band for button loops. Sew a button to end of underskirt band opposite buttonhole. Sew a button to end of veil band opposite buttonhole.
Waist Sash
Cut a piece of tulle 32"/81cm long and weave through spaces in Row 3 of skirt for waist sash.
Weave in any remaining ends.•

superhero dolls

Intermediate

MATERIALS
Yarn
RED HEART® Super Saver®, 7oz/198g, each approx 364yd/333m (acrylic)
• 1 skein each in Bright Yellow 324 (A), Turqua 512 (B), Pretty 'n Pink 722 (C), Spring Green 672 (D), and Amethyst 356 (E)

Hook
• Size H-8 (5mm) crochet hook, *or size to obtain gauge*

Notions
• Removable stitch markers
• Fifteen 5/8" buttons (8 for girl's outfit, 7 for boy's outfit)
• Yarn needle

FINISHED MEASUREMENTS
Both outfits fit 18"/45.5cm dolls
Girl's dress (chest circumference)
11"/27.5cm
Girl's dress (length) 9½"/24cm
Boy's pant suit (chest circumference)
11"/27.5cm
Boy's pant suit (length) 13"/33cm

GAUGE
16 sts = 4"/10cm; 16½ rows = 4"/10cm in single crochet using size H-8 (5mm) crochet hook.
CHECK YOUR GAUGE. Use any size hook to obtain the gauge.

superhero dolls

SPECIAL STITCHES
sc2tog [Pull up a loop in next st] twice, yarn over and draw through all 3 loops on hook.
dc2tog [Yarn over, insert hook in next stitch, yarn over and pull up loop, yarn over, draw through 2 loops] twice, yarn over, draw through all 3 loops on hook

SPECIAL TECHNIQUE
Chain Stitch Embroidery Thread yarn needle with indicated color, bring needle up through the fabric, *bring needle back down through the fabric in the same place, forming a yarn loop on outside of piece, bring needle up through the fabric about ¼"/.5cm away and through yarn loop, pull until loop is lying flat on fabric; repeat from * forming the desired line shape, bring needle down through the fabric just outside final loop, fasten off.

NOTES
1) To change color, work last stitch of old color to last yarn over. Yarn over with new color and draw through all loops on hook to complete stitch. Proceed with new color. Fasten off old color.
2) Girl's Dress and Boy's Pant Suit are each worked in one piece from the top down.

GIRL COSTUME
Body
With A, ch 37.
Row 1 (Right Side) Sc in 2nd ch from hook and in each ch across, turn—36 sc.
Row 2 Ch 1, sc in each of first 2 sc, ch 2 for buttonhole, skip next sc, sc in each of next 3 sc, 3 sc in next sc, mark center sc of 3 sc just made, sc in each of next 6 sc, 3 sc in next sc, mark center sc of 3 sc just made, sc in each of next 8 sc, 3 sc in next sc, mark center sc of 3 sc just made, sc in each of next 6 sc, 3 sc in next sc, mark center sc of 3 sc just made, sc in each of next 6 sc, turn—43 sc, 1 ch-2 space.
Row 3 Ch 1, *sc in each sc to marked sc, 3 sc in marked sc and move marker to center sc of 3 sc just made; repeat from * 3 more times, sc in each sc to ch-2 space, sc in ch-2 space, sc in each of last 2 sc, turn—52 sc.
Row 4 Ch 1, *sc in each sc to marked sc, 3 sc in marked sc and move marker to center sc of 3 sc just made; repeat from * 3 more times, sc in each sc to end, turn—60 sc.
Row 5 Repeat Row 4—68 sc.
Row 6 Ch 1, sc in each of first 2 sc, ch 2 for buttonhole, skip next sc, *sc in each sc to marked sc, 3 sc in marked sc and move marker to center sc of 3 sc just made; repeat from * 3 more times, sc in each sc to end, turn—76 sc.
Row 7 Repeat Row 3—84 sc.
Remove all markers.
Row 8 Ch 1, sc in each sc to end, turn.
Row 9 Ch 1, sc in each of first 12 sc, skip 19 sc for armhole, sc in each of next 22 sc, skip 19 sc for other armhole, sc in each of next 12 sc, turn – 46 sc.
Row 10 Ch 1, sc in each of first 2 sc, ch 2, skip next sc, sc in each sc to end, turn.
Row 11 Ch 1, sc in each sc to ch-2 space, sc in ch-2 space, sc in each of last 2 sc, turn.
Rows 12 and 13 Ch 1, sc in each sc to end, turn.
Row 14 Repeat Row 10.
Row 15 Repeat Row 11.
Row 16 Ch 1, sc in each sc to end, turn.
Change to B.
Row 17 Ch 1, sc in each sc to end, turn.
Row 18 Repeat Row 10.
Row 19 Repeat Row 11.
Fasten off.

Skirt
With Right Side facing, join C with a slip st in first st.
Row 1 (Right Side) Ch 2 (does not count as a st now and throughout), 2 dc in each sc to end, turn—92 dc.
Row 2 Ch 2, dc in each of first 2 dc, ch 1 for buttonhole, skip next dc, dc in each dc to end, turn—91 dc and 1 ch-1 space.
Row 3 Ch 2, dc in each dc to ch-1 space, dc in ch-1 space, dc in each of last 2 dc, turn.
Rows 4–7 Ch 2, dc in each dc to end, turn.
Fasten off.

Sleeves (make both the same)
With Wrong Side facing, join A with slip st in second underarm sc.
Row 1 (Wrong Side) Ch 1, sc in same sc as joining slip st, sc in each of next 19 armhole sc, sc in first underarm sc, turn—21 sc.
Row 2 Ch 1, sc in each sc to end, turn.
Row 3 Ch 1, sc2tog over first 2 sc, sc in each of next 17 sc, sc2tog over last 2 sc, turn—19 sc.
Rows 4–10 Repeat Row 2.
Change to B.
Rows 11 and 12 Repeat Row 2.
Fasten off.

Emblem
With C, ch 2.
Row 1 (Right Side) Ch 1, 3 sc in 2nd ch from hook, turn—3 sc.
Rows 2–7 Ch 1, sc in each sc to last sc, 2 sc in last sc, turn—9 sc.
Fasten off.

Edging
With Right Side facing, join B with slip st in any corner, ch 1, [2 sc in corner, 7 sc evenly spaced to next corner] 3 times, join with slip st in first sc.
Fasten off, leaving a long tail for sewing.
With A, embroider a chain st "S" on emblem.

Cape
With B, ch 51.
Row 1 (Right Side) Sc in 2nd ch from hook and in each ch to end, turn—50 sc.
Row 2 Ch 1, sc in each sc across, turn.
Row 3 Ch 2 (does not count as a st), dc in each sc across, turn.

superhero dolls

Row 4 Ch 1, sc in each dc across, turn
Rows 5–24 Repeat Rows 3 and 4 alternately.
Row 25 Repeat Row 3.
Row 26 Ch 1, sc in each of first 4 dc, sc2tog over next 2 dc, [sc in each of next 8 dc, sc2tog over next 2 dc] 4 times, sc in each of last 4 dc, turn—45 sc.
Row 27 Ch 2 (does not count as a st), dc in each of first 3 sc, dc2tog over next 2 sc, [dc in each of next 7 sc, dc2tog over next 2 sc] 4 times, dc in each of last 4 dc, turn—40 dc.
Row 28 Ch 1, sc in first dc, * sc2tog over next 2 dc, sc in next dc; repeat from * to end, turn—27 sc
Row 29 Ch 16 for button loop, sc in each sc to end.
Fasten off.

Armband
With C, ch 3.
Row 1 Sc in 2nd ch from hook and in next ch, turn—2 sc.
Rows 2–14 Ch 1, sc in each of 2 sc, turn.
Row 15 Ch 4 for button loop, skip first sc, join with slip st in 2nd sc.
Fasten off.

Boots
With B, ch 6.
Round 1 2 sc in 2nd ch from hook, sc in each of next 3 ch, 3 sc in next ch, working in back loops of foundation ch, sc in each of next 4 ch; join with slip st in first sc—12 sc.
Round 2 Ch 1, [sc in next sc, 2 sc in next sc, sc in each of next 3 sc, 2 sc in next sc] twice; join with slip st in first sc—16 sc.
Round 3 Ch 1, [sc in next sc, 2 sc in each of next 2 sc, sc in each of next 3 sc, 2 sc in each of next 2 sc] twice; join with slip st in first sc—24 sc.
Round 4 Ch 1, sc in back loop only of each sc around; join with slip st in first sc.
Rounds 5–7 Ch 1, sc in each sc around; join with slip st in first sc.
Round 8 Ch 1, sc in each of next 8 sc, [sc2tog over next 2 sc] 4 times, sc in each of next 8 sc; join with slip st in first sc—20 sc.
Round 9 Ch 1, sc in each of next 8 sc, [sc2tog over next 2 sc] twice, sc in each of next 8 sc; join with slip st in first sc—18 sc.
Round 10 Ch 1, sc in each of next 8 sc, sc2tog over next 2 sc, sc in each of next 8 sc, join with slip st in first sc—17 sc.
Rounds 11–18 Ch 1, sc in each sc around; join with slip st in first sc.
Fasten off.

BOY COSTUME

Shirt
With D, ch 37, and work Rows 1–12 same as Girl Costume.
Change to A, and work Rows 13–15 same as Girl Costume.

Pants
Change to E, and work Rows 16–19 same as Girl Costume.
Rows 20–24: Ch 1, sc in each sc to end, turn.

First Leg
Row 1 (Wrong Side) Slip st in each of first 4 sc for button flap, ch 1, 2 sc in next sc, sc in each of next 19 sc, 2 sc in next sc, mark next sc for beginning of opposite leg, turn—23 sc.
Change to D.
Rows 2 and 3 Ch 1, 2 sc in first sc, sc in each sc to last sc, 2 sc in next sc, turn—27 sc.
Rows 4 and 5 Ch 1, sc in each sc to end, turn.
Row 6 Ch 1, sc2tog over first 2 sc, sc in each sc to last 2 sc, sc2tog over last 2 sc, turn—25 sc.
Rows 7–28 Ch 1, sc in each sc to end, turn.
Fasten off.

Second Leg
Row 1 (Wrong Side) Join E with slip st in marked sc, remove marker, ch 1, 2 sc in same sc as joining slip st, sc in each of next 19 sts, 2 sc in next sc, turn—23 sc.
Change to D, and work Rows 2–28 same as first leg.
Fasten off.

Sleeves (Make 2)
Work same as sleeves of Girl Costume, using the following colors:
Rows 1–10 D.
Rows 11–12 E.
Fasten off.

Emblem
With E, work same as emblem of Girl Costume.

Edging
With A, work same as emblem edging of Girl Costume.
With D, embroider a chain st "S" on emblem.

Cape
With A, work same as cape of Girl Costume.

Armband
With A, work same as armband of Girl Costume.

Boots
With A, ch 6, and work Rounds 1–11 same as Boots of Girl Costume.
Round 12 Ch 1, 2 sc in first sc, [sc in each of next 5 sc, 2 sc in next sc] twice, sc in each of last 4 sc; join with slip st in first sc—20 sc.
Round 13–18 Ch 1, sc in each sc around; join with slip st in first sc. Fasten off.

FINISHING
Using photo as a guide, sew emblem to center of each shirt.
Sew 5 buttons to back of Boy Costume and 6 buttons to back of Girl Costume, corresponding with buttonholes.
Sew 1 button to end of each armband and 1 button to top corner of each cape, corresponding with button loops.
Sew sleeve seams of both outfits.
Sew leg seams of pants of Boy Costume, and sew down bottom of button flap.
Weave in all loose ends.•

33

nurse doll

Intermediate

MATERIALS
Yarn
RED HEART® Soft®, 5oz/141g balls, each approx 256yd/234m (acrylic)
- 1 ball each in 4600 White (A) and 5142 Cherry Red (B)
- 2 balls in 9520 Seafoam (C)

Hook
One each size G-6 (4mm) and I-9 (5.5mm), *or size to obtain gauge*

Notions
- Four ½"/13mm buttons
- Sewing needle and thread
- Yarn needle

FINISHED MEASUREMENTS
Dress fits 18"/45.5cm doll

GAUGE
12 sts = 4"/10cm; 15 rows = 4"10cm in single crochet with larger size hook.
CHECK YOUR GAUGE. Use any size hook to obtain the gauge.

SPECIAL STITCHES
dc2tog (double crochet 2 stitches together) [Yarn over, insert hook in next stitch, yarn over and pull up loop, yarn over, draw through 2 loops] 2 times, yarn over, draw through all 3 loops on hook.
Fpsc (front post single crochet) Insert hook from front to back and to front again around post of indicated stitch, yarn over and draw up a loop, yarn over and draw through 2 loops on your hook. Skip the stitch "behind" the Fpsc.
join with Fpsc Place slip knot on hook, work Fpsc around indicated stitch.
join with sc Place slipknot on hook, work sc in indicated stitch or space.

NOTES
1) Outfit includes 3 pieces: Hat, Dress, and Apron.
2) Bodice of Dress is worked is worked back and forth in rows from the waist upwards. Piece is divided at underarms and right back, front, and left back worked separately to shoulders.
3) Dress skirt is worked in joined and turned rounds from the waist downwards.
4) Sleeves are worked, directly into armhole openings, in joined and turned rounds.
5) Apron is worked in 4 pieces: Body, two Ties, and Front Cross. The pieces are sewn together to complete Apron.

HAT
With smaller hook and A, ch 2.
Row 1 (Right Side) Work 8 sc in 2nd ch from hook—8 sts.
Row 2 Ch 1, turn, 2 sc in each st across—16 sc.
Row 3 Ch 1, turn, [sc in next st, 2 sc in next st] 8 times—24 sc.
Row 4 Ch 1, turn, [sc in next 2 sts, 2 sc in next st] 8 times—32 sc.
Row 5 Ch 1, turn, [sc in next 3 sts, 2 sc in next st] 8 times—40 sc.
Row 6 Ch 1, turn, [sc in next 4 sts, 2 sc in next st] 8 times—48 sc.
Row 7 Ch 1, turn, sc in each st across.
Repeat Row 7 until piece measures about 3½"/9cm from beginning. Fasten off.

Front Flap
Row 1 Turn piece, skip first 6 sts, join A with Fpsc around next st, Fpsc around each of next 35 sts; leave remaining 6 sts unworked—36 Fpsc.
Row 2 Ch 1, turn, sc in each st across.
Repeat Row 2 until front flap measures about 2½"/6.5cm. Fasten off.
Fold flap back. With a double strand of B, embroider a straight stitch cross in middle of flap, sewing through both thicknesses to tack flap to hat. With A, sew back seam.

DRESS
Bodice
Beginning at waist, with larger hook and C, ch 40.
Row 1 (Right Side) Dc in 4th ch from hook (3 skipped ch count as first dc) and in each ch across—38 dc.

nurse doll

Row 2 Ch 3 (counts as first dc here and throughout), turn, dc in each st across.
Row 3 (button loop row) Ch 6 (button loop), turn, slip st in first dc, ch 3 (counts as dc), dc in each remaining st across—38 dc and 1 ch-6 button loop.
Rows 4 and 5 Repeat Rows 2 and 3.

Right Back
Row 6 (Wrong Side) Ch 3, turn, dc in next 6 sts; leave remaining 31 sts unworked—7 dc.
Rows 7–9 Ch 3, turn, dc in next 6 sts.
Fasten off.

Front
Row 6 (Wrong Side) With Wrong Side facing, skip next 5 unworked sts of Row 5 following right back for underarm, draw up a loop of C in next st, ch 3 (counts as dc), dc in next 13 sts; leave remaining 12 sts unworked—14 sts.
Rows 7–10 Ch 3, turn, dc in next 3 sts, hdc in next st, sc in next 4 sts, hdc in next st, dc in last 4 sts.
Fasten off.

Left Back
Row 6 (Wrong Side) With Wrong Side facing, skip next 5 unworked sts of Row 5 following front for underarm, draw up a loop of C in next st, ch 3 (counts as dc), dc in remaining 6 sts—7 dc.
Row 7 (button loop row) Ch 6 (button loop), turn, slip st in first dc, ch 3 (counts as dc), dc in each remaining st across—7 dc and 1 ch-6 button loop.
Row 8 Ch 3, turn, dc in each st across.
Row 9 Repeat Row 7.
Fasten off.

Shoulder Seams
Fold right back and left back over front. With C, sew shoulder seams, sewing tops of 4 double crochet stitches at each shoulder together.

SKIRT
With Right Side of bodice facing and larger hook, working across opposite side of bodice foundation chain, draw up a loop of C in first ch.
Round 1 (Right Side) Ch 3 (counts as dc here and throughout), dc in same ch as joining, 2 dc in each remaining ch across; join with slip st in top of beginning ch to begin working in rounds—76 dc.
Round 2 Ch 3, turn, 2 dc in next st, *dc in next st, 2 dc in next st; repeat from * around; join with slip st in top of beginning ch—114 dc.
Round 3 Ch 3, turn, dc in each st around; join with slip st in top of beginning ch.
Repeat Round 3 until skirt measures about 9"/23cm.
Fasten off.

SLEEVES (make 2)
With Right Side of bodice facing and larger hook, draw up a loop of C in center dc of one underarm.
Round 1 (Right Side) Ch 3 (counts as dc here and throughout), dc in next 2 sts; 2 dc in end of each of 9 rows around side edges of armhole, dc in remaining 2 sts of underarm; join with slip st in top of beginning ch—23 dc.
Rounds 2 and 3 Ch 3, turn, dc in each st around; join with slip st in top of beginning ch. Fasten off.

Cuff
With Wrong Side facing, draw up a loop of A in same st as joining.
Round 4 (Wrong Side) Ch 3, *dc in next st, dc2tog; repeat from * to last st, dc in last st; join with slip st in top of beginning ch—16 dc.
Round 5 Ch 3, dc in each st around; join with slip st in top of beginning ch.
Fasten off. Repeat for 2nd sleeve.

COLLAR
With Right Side facing and larger hook, draw up a loop of A at beginning of neck edge.
Row 1 (Right Side) Ch 3, work dc evenly spaced across neck edge.
Fasten off.

APRON
Skirt
With larger hook and A, ch 59.
Row 1 Dc in 4th ch from hook (3 skipped ch count as first dc) and in each ch across—57 dc.
Row 2 Ch 3 (counts as dc here and throughout), turn, dc in each st across.

Repeat Row 2 until piece measures about 7"/18cm from beginning.

Bib

Row 1 Ch 3, turn, *dc2tog; repeat from * across—29 dc.
Row 2 Ch 3, turn, [dc2tog] 14 times—15 dc.
Rows 3–9 Ch 3, turn, dc in each st across.
Fasten off.

Ties (make 2)

With larger hook, join A with sc in one end of Row 2 of bib, ch 71.
Row 1 Sc in 2nd ch from hook and in each ch across; slip st in end of Row 2 near joining sc.
Fasten off. Repeat for 2nd Tie, beginning at other end of Row 2 of bib.

Front Cross

With smaller hook and B, ch 5.

Ties (make 2) Center Bar

Row 1 Dc in 4th ch from hook (3 skipped ch count as first dc) and in last ch—3 dc.
Rows 2–5 Ch 3 (counts as dc here and throughout), turn, dc in next 2 sts.
Fasten off.

Cross Bar

Draw up a loop of B in one end of Row 3 of center bar.
Next Row Ch 3, 2 dc in same end of Row 3—3 dc.
Next 2 rows Ch 3, turn, dc in next 2 sts.
Fasten off. Repeat to work 2nd half of cross bar, beginning on other end of Row 3 of center bar. Fasten off, leaving a long tail for sewing.

FINISHING

With B, embroider a straight stitch cross in middle of each sleeve cuff. With sewing needle and thread, sew buttons opposite button loops.
With yarn tails, sew front cross to center of Apron bib.
Sew Apron bib to front bodice of Dress.
Weave in ends.•

mermaid doll

Easy

MATERIALS

Yarn
RED HEART® Super Saver®, 7oz/198g skeins, each approx 364yd/333m (acrylic) (4)
• 1 skein each in 530 Orchid (A), 722 Pretty 'n Pink (B), and 3862 Jade (C)

Hook
• Size I-9 (5.5mm) crochet hook, *or size to obtain gauge*

Notions
• Yarn needle

FINISHED MEASUREMENTS
Outfit fits 18"/45.5cm doll

GAUGE
12 sts = 4"/10cm; 8 rows of bodice = 2"/5cm using size I-9 (5.5mm) crochet hook.
CHECK YOUR GAUGE. Use any size hook to obtain the gauge.

SPECIAL STITCHES
dc2tog [Yarn over, insert hook in next stitch, yarn over and pull up loop, yarn over, draw through 2 loops] 2 times, yarn over, draw through all 3 loops on hook.
picot ch 4, slip st in 2nd ch from hook.
sc2tog [Insert hook in next stitch, yarn over and pull up a loop] twice, yarn over and draw through all 3 loops on hook.
sc3tog [Insert hook in next stitch, yarn over and pull up a loop] 3 times, yarn over and draw through all 4 loops on hook.

SPECIAL TECHNIQUE
Join with sc Place a slipknot on hook, insert hook in indicated stitch, yarn over and pull up a loop, yarn over and draw through both loops on hook.

NOTES
1) Bodice and body are worked back and forth in rows. Edges are sewn together from top of bodice to bottom of body. Fins are made separately and sewn to lower edge of body.
2) To change color, work last stitch of old color to last yarn over. Yarn over with new color and draw through all loops on hook to complete stitch. Proceed with new color. Cut old color.

OUTFIT
Bodice
With A, ch 34.
Row 1 (Right Side) Sc in 2nd ch from hook and in each ch across, turn—33 sc.
Rows 2–7 Ch 1, sc in each sc across, turn.
Row 8 Ch 1, sc in first 14 sc, skip next 2 sc, 5 dc in next sc, skip next 2 sc, sc in last 14 sc; change to B, turn—28 sc and 5 dc.
Row 9 Ch 1, sc in each st across to next dc, sc in next 2 dc, 3 sc in next dc, sc in each remaining st—32 sc and one 3-sc group. Fasten off, leaving long tail for sewing.

Strap
With B, ch 35, sc in center st of 3-sc group, ch 35. Fasten off.

Body
Row 1 (Right Side) With Right Side of bodice facing and working in opposite side of foundation row, join C with sc in first ch, sc in next 3 ch, *2 sc in next ch, sc in next 7 ch; repeat from * twice, 2 sc in next ch, sc in last 4 ch, turn—37 sc.
Row 2 Ch 1, sc in first sc, *skip next 2 sc, 5 dc in next sc, skip next 2 sc, sc in next sc; repeat from * across, turn—7 sc and 30 dc.
Row 3 Ch 3 (counts as first dc here and throughout), 2 dc in first sc, skip first 2 dc, sc in next dc, *skip next 2 dc, 5 dc in next sc, skip next 2 dc, sc in next dc; repeat from * across, skip last 2 dc, 3 dc in last sc, turn—6 sc and 31 dc.
Row 4 Ch 1, sc in first dc, skip next 2 dc, 5 dc in next sc, *skip next 2 dc, sc in next dc, skip next 2 dc, 5 dc in next sc; repeat from * across, skip last 2 dc, sc in top of beginning ch, turn—7 sc and 30 dc.

mermaid doll

Row 5 Repeat Row 3.
Rows 6–19 Repeat last 2 rows 7 times.
Row 20 Ch 1, sc in first 7 sc, [sc2tog] twice, sc in next 15 sc, [sc2tog] twice, sc in next 6 dc, sc in top of beginning ch, turn—33 sc.
Row 21 Ch 1, sc in first 6 sc, [sc2tog] twice, sc in next 13 sc, [sc2tog] twice, sc in last 6 sc, turn—29 sc.
Row 22 Ch 1, sc in first 5 sc, [sc2tog] twice, sc in next 11 sc, [sc2tog] twice, sc in last 5 sc, turn—25 sc.
Row 23 Ch 1, sc in first 4 sc, [sc2tog] twice, sc in next 9 sc, [sc2tog] twice, sc in last 4 sc, turn—21 sc.
Row 24 Ch 1, sc in first 3 sc, [sc2tog] twice, sc in next 7 sc, [sc2tog] twice, sc in last 3 sc, turn—17 sc.

Row 25 Ch 1, sc in first 2 sc, [sc2tog] twice, sc in next 5 sc, [sc2tog] twice, sc in last 2 sc, turn—13 sc.
Row 26 Ch 1, sc in first sc, [sc2tog] twice, sc in next 3 sc, [sc2tog] twice, sc in last sc, turn—9 sc.
Row 27 Ch 1, [sc2tog] twice, sc in next sc, [sc2tog] twice, turn—5 sc.
Row 28 Ch 1, sc2tog, sc in next sc, sc2tog, turn—3 sc.
Row 29 Ch 1, sc3tog—1 sc. Fasten off, leaving long tail for sewing.

First Fin
With B, leaving a long beginning tail, ch 17.
Row 1 (Right Side) Sc in 2nd ch from hook and in each ch across, turn—16 sc.
Row 2 Ch 3, dc in each sc across, turn.
Row 3 Ch 3, dc in next 7 dc; leave remaining dc unworked, turn—8 dc.
Row 4 Ch 3, dc2tog, dc in next 4 dc, dc in top of beginning ch, turn—7 dc.
Row 5 Ch 3, dc in next 3 sts, dc2tog, dc in top of beginning ch, turss dc.
Row 6 Ch 3, dc2tog, dc in next 2 dc, dc in top of beginning ch, turn—5 dc.
Row 7 Ch 3, dc in next dc, dc2tog, dc in top of beginning ch, turn—4 dc.
Row 8 Ch 3, dc2tog, dc in top of beginning ch, turn—3 dc.
Row 9 Ch 3, dc2tog, working 2nd "leg" in top of beginning ch, turn—2 dc. Fasten off.

Second Fin
Row 1 With Wrong Side of first fin facing, join B with slip st in top of beginning ch of Row 2, ch 3, dc in unworked 7 dc, turn—8 dc.
Rows 2–7 Repeat Rows 4–9 of first fin.

CROWN
With B, ch 33; join with slip st in first ch to form a ring.
Round 1 Ch 1, sc in each ch around; join with slip st in first sc—33 sc.
Round 2 Ch 1, sc in each sc around; join with slip st in first sc.
Round 3 Ch 1, sc in first sc, picot, *ch 3, skip next 2 sc, sc in next sc, picot; repeat from * around, ch 3; join in first sc—11 picots. Fasten off.

FINISHING
With end tails, sew matching edges of bodice and body together. Flatten lower section of body. Referring to photograph as a guide, with beginning tail, sew Row 1 of first fin to flattened edge of body. Weave in ends.•